Mindfulness and Mental Health

Staying Balanced and Focused in Your 40s and Beyond

Michelle Mann

Copyright © 2024 by Michelle Mann

All rights reserved.

No portion of this book may be reproduced in any form without written permission from the publisher or author, except as permitted by U.S. copyright law.

Contents

1. Introduction — 1
2. The Landscape of Midlife Mental Health — 3
3. Starting Your Mindfulness Journey — 8
4. Mindfulness Techniques for Everyday Life — 12
5. Cultivating Mindfulness in Relationships — 24
6. Mindfulness for Stress and Anxiety — 35
7. Mindful Approaches to Life's Challenges — 40
8. Mindfulness and Emotional Health — 47
9. Mindful Aging — 53
10. Advanced Mindfulness Practices — 56
11. Integrating Mindfulness into Your Legacy — 62

Introduction

♥

Welcome to *Mindfulness and Mental Health: Staying Balanced and Focused in Your 40s and Beyond.* Life beyond your 40s brings a unique set of anticipated and unexpected challenges. It's a time when you may find yourself juggling the demands of career, family, and personal growth, all while navigating the complexities of aging. This stage of life can be immensely rewarding but can also test your mental resilience.

We understand that you may be dealing with the pressures of a busy career, changing family dynamics, and the inevitable shifts in your physical and emotional well-being. But rest assured, this book is here to offer a guiding hand through it all. We firmly believe in the power of mindfulness to transform your mental health. Throughout these chapters, we'll explore how mindfulness can be your trusted ally, helping you maintain balance and focus no matter what life throws at you.

Above all, we aim to inspire and motivate you to commit to mindfulness practice, not as a chore but as a valuable tool for personal growth and mental clarity. By the end of this journey, you'll see mindfulness as a practice and a path to a healthier, more balanced, and focused life in your 40s and beyond. So, let's embark on this transformative journey together, where mindfulness becomes your steadfast companion on the road to improved mental health and well-being.

The Landscape of Midlife Mental Health

♥

Understanding Midlife Transitions. As you step into your 40s and beyond, you may traverse a landscape of profound changes and transitions. It's a phase of life where the familiar terrain of youth shifts, presenting you with new challenges and opportunities. At this juncture, it's perfectly normal to experience a whirlwind of emotions and thoughts, which often accompany these significant shifts. Here are some transitions many people in their 40s experience:

1. Career Changes: Many people in their 40s reassess their careers and may contemplate changing jobs or industries, pursuing further education or training, or even starting their own businesses.

2. Parenting Challenges: For those with children, the teenage years can bring new challenges as kids become more independent. Empty nest

syndrome can also be a significant emotional transition when children leave home for college or to start their own lives.

3. Marital and Relationship Shifts: Some individuals may experience changes in their marriages or long-term relationships, such as divorce or the need to rekindle the romance as children become less dependent.

4. Health and Well-being: Health concerns and the realization of aging may prompt people to adopt healthier lifestyles, including exercise, diet changes, and regular medical check-ups.

5. Financial Planning: People in their 40s often focus more on long-term financial planning, such as saving for retirement, paying off debts, and making investments.

6. Empty Nest and Parenting Roles: As children grow up and move out, parents may need to redefine their roles and rediscover their own interests and passions.

7. Self-Identity and Self-Discovery: Many individuals use their 40s as a time to reflect on their life choices, values, and goals, leading to personal growth and self-discovery.

8. Caregiving Responsibilities: Some may find themselves caring for aging parents or family members, which can be emotionally and physically demanding.

9. Reevaluating Priorities: Midlife often prompts individuals to reassess their priorities and focus on what truly matters to them, whether it's relationships, personal goals, or giving back to the community.

10. Social Changes: Friendships may evolve as people in their 40s connect with others who share their interests or life stages.

11. Menopause and Aging: Women often go through menopause in their 40s, which can come with its own set of physical and emotional changes.

12. Midlife Crisis: Some individuals experience a midlife crisis, characterized by a period of questioning, anxiety, and seeking new experiences or changes in life direction.

Whew! What a list! You may be embracing the joys of a maturing family while simultaneously grappling with the sense of an impending empty nest. Career trajectories may plateau or take unexpected turns. Your body may exhibit signs of aging that you hadn't anticipated. And amidst it all, the pressures and responsibilities can sometimes feel overwhelming.

Common mental health challenges associated with midlife include depression, often triggered by life changes and a sense of unfulfillment, leading to persistent sadness and loss of interest. Anxiety, heightened by increased responsibilities, can manifest as excessive worry, restlessness, and physical symptoms. Empty Nest Syndrome can evoke feelings of loneliness when children leave home, while identity crises prompt existential questioning and potential confusion. Relationship struggles may result from marital issues or communication problems, and caregiver stress often accompanies caring for aging family members. Existential concerns emerge as people confront mortality, and some individuals experience midlife crises marked by impulsive behavior and discontent, often requiring professional help.

Know that these feelings are not yours alone. Many individuals experience these midlife transitions, and it's crucial to address the mental health challenges that can arise from them. It's important to note that these midlife transitions are not universal, and individuals may experience them in different ways and at different times. Some individuals may navigate this period relatively easily, while others may face significant challenges. What's common is the opportunity for self-discovery, growth, and the potential for a more fulfilling life in the years ahead.

The Science of Mindfulness. Mindfulness is not just a buzzword; it's a scientifically validated approach to mental well-being. It offers a beacon of hope and a toolkit of techniques to help you navigate the challenges of midlife with clarity and purpose. Scientific studies have shown that mindfulness practices can reduce stress, improve emotional regulation, enhance self-awareness, and increase resilience. These benefits are not merely theoretical but have been experienced and celebrated by countless individuals like you who have embarked on this mindful journey.

Mindfulness practices have gained significant attention in scientific research, and a growing body of evidence supports their benefits, including for people in their 40s and beyond. Research indicates that regular mindfulness meditation can lower cortisol levels (a stress hormone), decrease perceived stress, and improve overall well-being. Managing stress is particularly relevant for individuals in their 40s who may face increased responsibilities and demands.

Mindfulness practices also enhance emotional regulation. Studies have demonstrated that mindfulness can help individuals better manage their emotions, reduce symptoms of anxiety and depression, and increase emotional resilience, all of which are beneficial in midlife and beyond. Also, mindfulness meditation has been associated with improved cognitive functions such as attention, memory, and executive functioning. These cognitive enhancements are valuable as individuals age and may face cognitive challenges.

Furthermore, studies show mindfulness fosters self-awareness, self-reflection, and positive aging. Practicing mindfulness allows individuals to become more attuned to their thoughts, emotions, and behaviors, aiding in personal growth and self-improvement. Mindfulness can promote positive aging outcomes by encouraging a positive mindset about aging, reducing age-related stress, and contributing to psychological well-being as people move through their 40s and beyond. Some studies suggest that mindfulness practices contribute to longevity by promoting healthier lifestyle choices, reducing stress-related health issues, and enhancing overall physical and mental health.

Mindfulness practices have also been linked to improved physical health outcomes, including better cardiovascular health, reduced inflammation, and enhanced immune system functioning. These benefits can contribute to overall well-being as individuals age. Mindfulness-based interventions have even been effective in reducing chronic pain and improving pain-related quality of life. Managing pain is especially relevant for individuals dealing with age-related health issues.

Starting Your Mindfulness Journey

♥

Embarking on your mindfulness journey is an exciting and transformative step towards improved mental health. In this chapter, we'll lay the foundation by introducing you to the basics of mindfulness practices designed with beginners in mind. Whether you're entirely new to mindfulness or have some experience, these practices will serve as a gentle entry point.

At its core, mindfulness is about being fully present in the moment without judgment. It's the art of embracing each moment just as it is, without rushing or wishing it were different. We'll guide you through simple techniques to help you develop this profound skill.

We emphasize the importance of consistency in your practice. Like any other skill, mindfulness improves with practice and dedication.

Setting realistic expectations for yourself is vital; it's okay if your mind occasionally wanders or if you find it challenging in the beginning. The journey of mindfulness is about progress, not perfection.

Creating a Mindful Environment. Your surroundings play a significant role in nurturing your mindfulness practice. This section offers practical tips for creating an environment conducive to mindfulness in your daily life. Mindfulness need not be time-consuming; it can seamlessly integrate into your daily routines, making it accessible to even the busiest of people. As you embark on this journey, remember that mindfulness is not an all-or-nothing commitment. Small, mindful moments sprinkled throughout your day can significantly impact your mental health.

Creating a mindful environment involves setting up a space that promotes a sense of calm, presence, and inner peace. Whether you're establishing a dedicated mindfulness corner in your home or infusing mindfulness into your daily surroundings, here are some steps to help you create a mindful environment:

1. Choose a Quiet Space: Select a quiet and peaceful area to practice mindfulness without distractions. It could be a corner of your living room, a spare room, or even a cozy spot in your backyard. Ensure that this space feels comfortable and inviting.

2. Declutter and Simplify: Remove unnecessary clutter and distractions from your chosen space. A clutter-free environment can contribute to mental clarity and focus. Simplify the décor to create a sense of tranquility.

3. Comfortable Seating: Invest in comfortable seating like a

cushion, chair, or meditation bench. Your seating should support an upright but relaxed posture, allowing you to sit comfortably for extended periods.

4. Natural Elements: Bring in natural elements such as plants, flowers, or natural materials like wood or stone. Nature can have a calming and grounding effect, enhancing the mindfulness experience.

5. Soft Lighting: Opt for soft, natural lighting. Consider using candles, soft lamps, or dimmer switches to create a soothing atmosphere. Avoid harsh, bright lights that can be jarring to the senses.

6. Mindfulness Props: Depending on your mindfulness practices, you may include props like a meditation cushion, yoga mat, or essential oils for aromatherapy.

7. Sensory Elements: Engage multiple senses. Use soothing scents like lavender or eucalyptus, calming sounds like soft music or nature sounds, and tactile items like textured cushions or prayer beads.

8. Mindful Decor: Decorate your space with items that inspire mindfulness. This could include artwork, quotes, or symbols that hold personal significance and remind you of the present moment.

9. Try to Stay Organized and Tidy: Keep the space organized and tidy. Make it a habit to put away any props or items after your practice to maintain a clutter-free environment.

10. Personalize It: Make the space your own by personalizing it

with meaningful items. It should feel like a sanctuary where you can connect with yourself.

Wherever you choose to set up your space, consider making it a technology-free zone to minimize distractions. Turn off phones, tablets, and other electronics during your mindful practice. Also, dedicate time for regular maintenance of your mindful environment. This could include cleaning, dusting, and refreshing the space to keep it inviting.

Remember that your mindful environment should resonate with you. It's a place where you can retreat to find stillness and presence. Over time, as you establish and maintain this space, it will become a haven for your mindfulness practice, helping you cultivate a greater sense of peace and clarity in your daily life.

Mindfulness Techniques for Everyday Life

♥

In this chapter, we dive deeper into the heart of mindfulness by exploring two foundational practices: breathwork and meditation. These techniques are essential tools in your mindfulness toolkit, and you can seamlessly integrate them into your daily life to foster a greater sense of balance and clarity. Both practices help reduce stress and anxiety, promoting relaxation and a sense of inner calm. They can enhance focus and concentration, improve sleep quality, and boost mental clarity. Additionally, breathwork and meditation contribute to better self-awareness, emotional regulation, and a greater sense of mindfulness, enabling individuals to navigate life's challenges with greater resilience and stability. Regular practice of these techniques can improve physical health, such as lowered blood pressure and enhanced immune function, making them valuable tools for holistic wellness and personal growth.

1. Find a Quiet Space: Choose a quiet and comfortable space where you won't be disturbed. Sit or lie down in a relaxed posture.

2. Mindful Awareness: Begin by bringing your attention to your breath. Observe your natural breathing pattern without trying to change it. Notice the rhythm, depth, and sensations of your breath.

3. Diaphragmatic Breathing (Deep Belly Breathing): Start with diaphragmatic breathing, which involves engaging your diaphragm to breathe deeply into your belly. Here's how to do it:

- Place one hand on your chest and the other on your abdomen.

- Inhale slowly through your nose, allowing your abdomen to rise as you fill your lungs with air. Your chest should remain relatively still.

- Exhale slowly and completely through your mouth or nose, allowing your abdomen to fall.

- Continue this deep, slow breathing pattern for several breaths.

1. Box Breathing (4-4-4-4): This technique helps regulate and deepen your breath. Inhale, hold, exhale, and hold for four seconds each. Here's how to do it:

- Inhale slowly through your nose for a count of four.

- Hold your breath for a count of four.

- Exhale slowly and completely through your mouth or nose for a count of four.

- Hold your breath at the bottom of your exhale for a count of four.

- Repeat this cycle for several rounds.

  1. Alternate Nostril Breathing (Nadi Shodhana): This yogic breathwork technique balances the body's energy flow and promotes a sense of calm. Here's how to do it:

- Sit comfortably with your spine straight.

- Use your right thumb to close off your right nostril and your right ring finger to close off your left nostril.

- Start by closing your right nostril and inhaling slowly and deeply through your left nostril.

- After inhaling, close your left nostril with your ring finger, release your right nostril, and exhale slowly through your right nostril.

- Inhale through your right nostril.

- Close your right nostril, release your left nostril, and exhale through your left nostril.

- Repeat this cycle, starting with the left nostril, for several rounds.

  1. Mindful Breath Observation: Return to mindful breath observation after practicing specific techniques. Pay attention to changes in your breath, your body's sensations, and your mind's state.

  2. Lengthen and Deepen Your Breath: Gradually lengthen and deepen your breath as you feel comfortable. You can increase the duration of each breath cycle or continue with the spe-

cific technique you prefer.

3. Practice Regularly: Consistency is key. Set aside time each day to practice breathwork, even if it's just for a few minutes. Over time, you may notice increased relaxation, reduced stress, and improved mental clarity.

Breathwork is versatile, and different techniques may be more suitable for specific goals or situations. Experiment with various methods and find the ones most resonating with you. Whether you use breathwork for relaxation, stress reduction, or as part of a mindfulness practice, it can become a valuable tool for enhancing your overall well-being.

Meditation. Meditation is a cornerstone of mindfulness practice. We'll provide you with short, guided meditation scripts that you can use for daily practice. These meditations are carefully crafted to help you develop mindfulness skills gradually, starting with the basics and progressing to more advanced techniques.

Through meditation, you'll learn to observe your thoughts and emotions without judgment, creating space for clarity and self-awareness. You'll discover that meditation is not about emptying your mind but embracing it with compassion and understanding.

Mindful Movement. Incorporating physical activity into your mindfulness practice can be a game-changer. This section introduces you to gentle, mindful movement practices like yoga and tai chi. These practices blend physical activity with mindfulness, offering a holistic approach to well-being.

Mindful movement in one's 40s can take various forms, and it involves integrating physical activity with mindfulness principles to promote awareness, presence, and well-being. Here's what mindful movement can look like in your 40s and how you can incorporate it into your daily life for mindfulness practice:

- **Yoga.** Yoga is a well-known form of mindful movement. Practicing yoga involves a combination of physical postures, breath control, and meditation. Yoga promotes flexibility, strength, and relaxation while encouraging mindfulness by emphasizing the connection between movement and breath. Yoga is a holistic practice that can significantly enhance mental clarity and increase emotional stability. Combining physical postures, breath control, and meditation techniques in yoga fosters a mind-body connection that supports mental well-being. Through asanas (physical poses), practitioners increase awareness of their body, release physical tension, and improve circulation. This physical aspect of yoga can alleviate stress and anxiety, allowing the mind to become more centered and clear. Consider attending yoga classes or using online resources to practice yoga at home. Even short, daily sessions can significantly impact your physical and mental well-being.

- **Tai Chi.** Tai Chi, a traditional Chinese martial art characterized by slow, flowing movements and deep breathing, can significantly enhance mental clarity and increase emotional stability. The practice involves a strong mind-body connection and mindfulness, which can contribute to these benefits. Tai Chi demands focused attention on the precise execution of movements and the coordination of breath, leading to improved concentration and mental clarity. Over time, this mindful engagement can help quiet the chatter of a busy mind, reduce mental distractions, and enhance cognitive function. The deliberate and slow-paced nature of Tai Chi also encourages practitioners to be present in the moment, fostering a sense of clarity and heightened awareness. Tai Chi promotes emotional stability through its emphasis on relaxation and stress reduction. The slow, controlled movements can trigger the body's relaxation response, reducing the production of stress hormones like cortisol. Regular practice can help individuals better manage daily stressors and emotional challenges.One can incorporate Tai Chi by looking for local Tai Chi classes or instructional videos online. Practicing Tai Chi in a park or natural setting can enhance the sense of mindfulness and connection to nature.

- **Walking Meditation.** Walking meditation is a mindfulness practice that combines the physical activity of walking with the meditative aspect of focused attention. When practicing walking meditation, individuals concentrate on each step, their breath, and the sensations of movement, grounding themselves in the present moment. This heightened awareness helps quiet the mind, reduce mental clutter, and improve cognitive clarity. It lets individuals release racing thoughts, worries, and distractions, promoting a clearer and calmer mental state.By paying attention to their thoughts and feelings while walking, individuals can identify and acknowledge any emotional turmoil or stress they might be experiencing. This awareness empowers them to address these emotions more effectively, fostering emotional resilience and a greater sense of calm. Over time, practicing walking meditation regularly can lead to a more balanced emotional state and a stronger ability to navigate life's challenges with composure and equanimity, ultimately enhancing overall mental and emotional well-being. Incorporating daily walking meditation into your routine is a great way to reap its benefits. Here's a step-by-step guide to help you get started:

1. Choose a time: Pick a convenient time for your walking meditation. It could be in the morning to start your day with clarity or during a lunch break to refresh your mind. Consistency is key, so select a time that suits your daily schedule.

2. Find a peaceful location: Select a quiet and safe place to walk where you won't be easily distracted by traffic or other people. It could be a park, a garden, or a peaceful neighborhood street.

3. Dress comfortably: Wear comfortable clothing and appropriate footwear for walking, ensuring you can move freely and comfortably.

4. Begin with mindful preparation: Before you start walking, take a few moments to stand still and ground yourself. Take a few deep breaths, focusing on your inhales and exhales. Set an intention for your meditation, such as cultivating mindfulness or reducing stress.

5. Start walking slowly: Start walking slower than your usual stride. Maintain a natural and relaxed posture, keeping your head up and eyes open, gazing a few feet ahead of you.

6. Pay attention to your steps: Focus on each step as you walk. Notice the sensation of your feet lifting, moving, and touching the ground. You can silently repeat a simple phrase like "step by step" with your footsteps to help maintain focus.

7. Be aware of your breath: Coordinate your breath with your steps. Inhale for a certain number of steps, and then exhale for the same number of steps. This synchronization can deepen your mindfulness during the practice.

8. Embrace distractions: If your mind starts to wander or if distractions arise, acknowledge them without judgment and gently return your focus to walking and breathing.

9. Set a duration: Decide how long you want to practice walking meditation. It could be as short as 10-15 minutes or longer if you prefer. Use a timer or a meditation app if needed.

10. Transition mindfully: When your meditation time is up, slow down your walking and come to a standstill. Take a few moments to reflect on your experience, express gratitude for the practice, and carry a sense of mindfulness with you as you continue with your day.

Mindful Stretching

Incorporate mindful stretching routines into your daily life. Stretching can help alleviate tension, improve flexibility, and promote relaxation. Mindful stretching is a practice that combines the physical benefits of stretching exercises with the principles of mindfulness meditation. It involves paying close attention to the sensations, movements, and breath during stretching, fostering a deeper mind-body connection and relaxation. Incorporating mindful stretching into your daily routine can promote physical flexibility, reduce muscle tension, and enhance overall well-being. Set aside a specific time for mindful stretching in your daily schedule. It could be in the morning to wake up your body and mind or in the evening to unwind and release the tension built up during the day. Find a quiet and comfortable space where you won't be easily disturbed. Begin with a few deep breaths to center yourself. As you move into your stretches, focus on the sensations in your body. Feel the stretch in your muscles, notice any tension or discomfort, and breathe deeply and naturally. Avoid pushing yourself too hard; aim for gentle and gradual movements that respect your body's limitations. While stretching, maintain your awareness of each movement and the corresponding sensations. If your mind wanders, gently bring your focus back to the present moment and your body. You can use a soft and soothing mantra or affirmation to enhance your mindfulness, such as "I am present" or "I am releasing tension." Incorporate a variety of stretches that target different muscle groups, and take your time with each one. After your stretching session, take a moment to acknowledge the benefits of your practice, express gratitude for the self-care, and carry the sense of relaxation and mindfulness with you for the rest of your day.Mindful stretching can be a valuable addition to your daily routine, promoting physical health and mental well-being by fostering a deeper connection between your mind and body while allowing you to release tension and stress.

Body Scan Meditation

Body scan meditation is a mindfulness practice that systematically focuses your attention on different body parts, from head to toe or vice versa. It aims to increase awareness of bodily sensations, reduce tension, and promote relaxation. Here's how you can incorporate it into your daily routine:

1. Find a quiet space: Choose a peaceful environment where you can comfortably lie down or sit. Make sure you won't be disturbed during your practice, and dim the lights if it helps create a calming atmosphere.

2. Get into a comfortable position: You can practice body scan meditation, either lying down with your arms by your sides or sitting in a comfortable chair with your feet flat on the ground. Close your eyes if you feel comfortable doing so.

3. Start with mindful breathing: Begin your session by taking a few deep breaths to center yourself and bring awareness to the present moment. Inhale deeply through your nose, hold briefly, and exhale slowly through your mouth.

4. Begin the scan: Start at the top of your head or your toes – either direction works. Imagine a warm and gentle spotlight of awareness moving slowly through your body, section by section. As you focus on each area, notice any sensations, tensions, or discomfort without judgment.

5. Breathe and release: As you scan each body part, take a few slow, deep breaths into that area. With each exhale, visualize any tension or discomfort melting away, allowing that part of your body to relax.

6. Progress systematically: Continue moving your attention down or up your body, section by section. Common focus points include the scalp, forehead, face, neck, shoulders, chest, arms, back, abdomen, hips, thighs, knees, calves, ankles, and feet.

7. Be patient and non-judgmental: If your mind wanders or you notice any discomfort or tension, acknowledge it without self-criticism and gently guide your attention back to the body scan.

8. Complete the scan: Once you have scanned your entire body, take a few moments to rest in a state of full-body awareness. Feel the sense of relaxation and calmness that the practice has cultivated.

9. Gradually return: When you're ready to conclude your session, gradually become aware of your surroundings. Start by wiggling your fingers and toes, then gently open your eyes. Take your time before getting up to allow the benefits of the practice to linger.

Incorporating body scan meditation into your daily routine can help alleviate stress, improve body awareness, and promote relaxation. You can practice for as little as 10-15 minutes or extend time to suit your preferences. Many people find that doing it in the morning or before bed helps set a positive tone for the day or ensures a restful night's sleep. Consistency is always key, so try to make it a daily habit to experience the full range of benefits over time.

Another way one can include mindful movement is through everyday activities. For example, gardening is a mindful movement activity that allows you to connect with nature, focus on the present moment, and engage your senses. Spending time tending to your garden, paying attention to the sensation of digging, planting, and nurturing plants can be a meditative, rewarding experience.

Cooking, cleaning, or even doing the dishes are ways to incorporate mindful movement.. Pay attention to the sensory experiences, movements, and sensations involved in these tasks. Approach these activities as opportunities for mindfulness. Engage your senses fully, notice the textures, smells, and movements involved, and be present in the moment. To incorporate mindful movement into your daily life, start with small steps and gradually build it into your routine. Mindful movement not only enhances physical health but also deepens your mindfulness practice, allowing you to stay present, reduce stress, and appreciate the richness of each moment, particularly as you navigate the challenges and opportunities of your 40s and beyond.

Whether you choose to focus on breathwork, meditation, or mindful movement, these techniques will empower you to infuse mindfulness into your everyday life. They will become your allies in navigating the challenges of midlife with grace and resilience, allowing you to maintain balance and focus even in the midst of life's complexities. As you explore these practices, remember that mindfulness is a journey of self-discovery, and each moment of awareness brings you closer to a more fulfilled and centered life.

Cultivating Mindfulness in Relationships

♥

Your journey of mindfulness extends beyond the boundaries of your inner self; it also holds the power to transform your relationships. In this chapter, we delve into the art of mindful communication, which can profoundly impact your connections with partners, family members, colleagues, and friends.

Incorporating Mindfulness into Communication. Mindful communication is about being fully present and attentive when engaging with others, whether in everyday interactions or in challenging situations. Mindfulness in communicating with others is a valuable skill that enhances the quality of your interactions, fosters better understanding, and promotes positive relationships. Here are some steps and techniques to help you incorporate mindfulness into your communication:

1. Practice Active Listening:

- When someone is speaking to you, give them your full attention.

- Avoid interrupting or formulating your response while they are talking.

- Show that you are listening by nodding, making eye contact, and providing verbal cues like "I see" or "I understand."

2. Stay Present in the Conversation:

- Focus on the current moment and the person you are communicating with.

- Let go of distractions and preoccupations, allowing yourself to fully engage in the conversation.

3. Mindful Breathing:

- Use your breath to stay centered during conversations.

- If you feel tension or emotional reactivity rising, take a few deep, conscious breaths to calm your mind before responding.

4. Non-Judgmental Awareness:

- Approach the conversation with an open and non-judgmental attitude.

- Suspend judgment and assumptions, allowing the speaker to express themselves without feeling criticized.

5. Empathetic Listening:

- Try to understand the speaker's perspective and emotions.

- Imagine yourself in their shoes to cultivate empathy and compassion.

6. Reflective Responses:

- Before responding, take a moment to reflect on what was said.

- Offer responses that acknowledge the speaker's feelings and experiences. For example, "I can see why you might feel that way."

7. Ask Open-Ended Questions:

- Encourage meaningful dialogue by asking open-ended questions that invite the speaker to share more deeply.

- Avoid questions that can be answered with a simple "yes" or "no."

8. Mindful Speech:

- Be aware of your own speech and its impact on others.

- Speak with kindness and consideration, avoiding harsh or hurtful words.

9. Pause Before Reacting:

- If you feel strong emotions rising during a conversation, take a moment to pause and collect your thoughts before responding impulsively.

10. Practice Compassionate Communication:

- Use "I" statements to express your thoughts and feelings without blaming or accusing others. For example, say "I felt hurt when..." instead of "You hurt me when..."

- Avoid making sweeping judgments or generalizations about the other person's character or intentions.

11. Body Language Awareness:

- Pay attention to your body language, as it communicates a lot about your engagement in the conversation.

- Maintain an open posture and avoid crossed arms or defensive gestures.

12. Mindful Endings:

- Conclude the conversation mindfully by summarizing key points and expressing gratitude for the exchange.

- Leave room for further discussion if needed.

13. Self-Compassion:

- Be gentle with yourself if you make mistakes in communication. Mindfulness is a practice, and it's okay to learn and improve over time.

Incorporating mindfulness into communication requires ongoing practice and self-awareness. It can lead to more meaningful, authentic, and empathetic connections with others. By cultivating mindfulness in your interactions, you create an environment that promotes understanding and harmony in your relationships, both personally and professionally.

Real-Life Scenarios and Scripts

To help you apply these principles in your life, we'll present real-life scenarios and scripts for practicing mindful communication. These examples will illustrate how mindfulness can diffuse conflicts, improve active listening, and create an atmosphere of trust and respect in your relationships. Through mindful communication, you'll discover the power of words and presence in nurturing healthy and meaningful connections with the people in your life.

Scenario 1: Conflict Resolution with a Coworker–You and a co-worker have differing opinions on how to approach a project, and the conversation is escalating into a conflict.

- **Step 1**: Acknowledge Emotions Mindfully

- Take a moment to pause and collect your thoughts.

- Acknowledge any emotions you are experiencing, such as frustration or irritation.

- **Step 2**: Active Listening and Empathy

- Practice active listening by giving your co-worker your full attention.

- Let your co-worker express their perspective without interruption.

- Show empathy by acknowledging their point of view and emotions.

Example Script: "I hear your concerns about the project, and I understand that you have a different approach in mind. It seems like you're feeling strongly about this, and I appreciate your input."

- **Step 3**: Express Your Perspective Mindfully

- When it's your turn to speak, express your thoughts and feelings thoughtfully and respectfully.

Example Script: "I value your input, and I also have some thoughts I'd like to share. I believe that our differing perspectives can be beneficial, and I'd like us to find a solution that takes both viewpoints into account."

- **Step 4**: Seek Common Ground

- Explore potential areas of agreement or compromise.

Example Script: "Are there aspects of both approaches that we can incorporate into a solution? Perhaps we can find a middle ground that benefits the project."

- **Step 5**: Mindful Closure

- Conclude the conversation with a mindful approach, expressing your commitment to working together towards a resolution.

Example Script: "Thank you for discussing this with me. I appreciate your input, and I'm committed to finding a solution that works for both of us. Let's continue this conversation and collaborate to reach our project goals."

Scenario 2: Family Discussion on Household Responsibilities–You and your family members are having a discussion about sharing household responsibilities, and the conversation is becoming tense.

- **Step 1**: Ground Yourself Mindfully

- Take a moment to ground yourself through a few deep breaths.

- Release any tension in your body.

- **Step 2**: Active Listening and Empathy

- Listen to each family member's perspective without judgment.

- Show empathy by acknowledging their feelings and experiences.

Example Script: "I hear that you're feeling overwhelmed with your responsibilities, and I understand how that can be frustrating."

- **Step 3**: Express Your Needs Mindfully

- Share your own perspective and needs with mindfulness.

Example Script: "I also have some concerns about the division of responsibilities, and I believe it's important for us to work together as a family to find a fair and sustainable solution."

- **Step 4**: Brainstorm Solutions Together

- Collaboratively brainstorm solutions that take everyone's needs into account.

Example Script: "Can we brainstorm together and come up with a plan that ensures fairness and balance in our household chores?"

- **Step 5**: Mindful Closure

- Conclude the conversation by expressing your commitment to finding a resolution together.

Example Script: "Thank you for discussing this with me. I'm grateful that we can have open conversations as a family. Let's continue working together to create a harmonious and supportive home environment."

In both scenarios, practicing mindful communication involves staying present, active listening, empathy, and a willingness to collaborate toward a mutually beneficial solution. Mindful scripts help facilitate respectful and constructive conversations, even in challenging situations.

Building Empathy and Compassion

Empathy and compassion play crucial roles in mindful practices and communication, particularly for individuals in their 40s and beyond who have accumulated life experiences and often find themselves navigating complex social and emotional dynamics. These qualities are essential in fostering meaningful connections and promoting personal growth and well-being.

Empathy involves the ability to understand and share the feelings of others, and it's a foundational element of mindful communication. As people in their 40s and beyond face a wide range of life challenges, including career transitions, family responsibilities, and personal growth, empathy becomes essential in acknowledging and validating the emotions of those they interact with. By actively listening and trying to see the world from the perspective of others, individuals in this age group can build stronger relationships with family, friends, and colleagues. Empathy helps bridge generational gaps in understanding and fosters a sense of connection and support, which can be especially valuable as one gets older and relies more on social networks for emotional well-being.

Compassion, on the other hand, goes beyond understanding and extends to a genuine desire to alleviate suffering or offer support. It involves kindness, forgiveness, and a willingness to help others in times of need. For individuals in their 40s and beyond, compassion becomes a powerful tool for managing the challenges that come with middle age and beyond. Whether it's caring for aging parents, dealing with health issues, or navigating career changes, the ability to approach these situations with compassion, both for oneself and for others, can reduce stress and promote resilience. Compassionate communication can create a more supportive and harmonious environment, allowing individuals to face life's complexities with a greater sense of purpose and positivity.

Developing empathy and compassion is an ongoing process that can greatly benefit individuals in their 40s and beyond. Here are some exercises and practices to help cultivate these qualities:

1. Mindful Listening: Set aside time to engage in deep, empathetic listening with someone close to you—a friend, family member, or colleague. Focus on their words, emotions, and body language without offering solutions or judgments. Allow them to express themselves fully while you provide a safe and empathetic space.

2. Journaling: Keep a gratitude journal where you write down daily moments of kindness and compassion you've witnessed or experienced. Reflect on the positive impact these actions had on you and others. This exercise can help you become more attuned to acts of compassion in your life.

3. Self-Compassion Meditation: Practice self-compassion through meditation. Spend time each day sending kind and compassionate

thoughts to yourself, especially during challenging moments. Recognize that it's okay to have difficulties and treat yourself with the same kindness you would offer to a friend.

4. Perspective-Taking: Challenge your biases and assumptions by actively trying to see situations from someone else's perspective. This could involve imagining what it's like to walk in their shoes, considering their background and experiences, and reflecting on how those factors influence their actions and emotions.

5. Random Acts of Kindness: Make an effort to perform small acts of kindness regularly, whether helping a neighbor, volunteering, or simply offering a kind word to someone in need. These actions can increase your compassion and create a positive ripple effect in your community.

6. Compassion Meditation: Engage in loving-kindness or compassion meditation exercises, sending wishes for happiness, health, and well-being to yourself, loved ones, acquaintances, and even people you may have conflicts with. Gradually expand the circle of compassion to encompass all living beings.

7. Compassionate Self-Talk: Pay attention to your inner dialogue. Whenever you notice self-criticism or negative self-talk, consciously replace it with more self-compassionate and supportive language. Treat yourself with the same understanding and encouragement you would offer to a friend.

8. Story Sharing: Connect with others in your age group or community to share personal stories of compassion and empathy. This can create a supportive environment for discussing and learning from each other's experiences.

9. Volunteer Work: Engage in volunteer activities or join community organizations that focus on helping people in need. Participating in such activities can deepen your understanding of others' struggles and inspire greater compassion.

10. Mindful Compassion Breaks: Throughout your day, take short breaks to pause, breathe deeply, and consciously generate feelings of compassion. Offer well-wishes for yourself and others, particularly in moments of stress or frustration.

Remember that developing empathy and compassion is an ongoing journey. Be patient with yourself and practice these exercises regularly to cultivate these qualities, ultimately leading to more meaningful and harmonious relationships, both with others and with yourself, as you enter and navigate your 40s and beyond.

Mindfulness for Stress and Anxiety

♥

Entering your 40s and beyond can bring about various stressors, both physical and emotional, that manifest differently for each individual. Physically, stress in this age group can lead to a range of symptoms. Some may experience increased muscle tension, particularly in the neck and shoulders, leading to headaches or even migraines. Sleep disturbances become more common, with difficulties falling asleep or staying asleep, and may contribute to fatigue. Skin issues, such as breakouts or exacerbation of skin conditions like psoriasis or eczema, can also be stress-related. Gastrointestinal problems like irritable bowel syndrome (IBS) may worsen or flare up due to heightened stress levels. Weight gain or changes in appetite can occur as stress affects eating habits and metabolism.

Emotionally, stress in your 40s and beyond may manifest as increased anxiety and worry about various life aspects. Many individuals in this age group face financial concerns, especially related to retirement planning and supporting children or aging parents, leading to chronic anxiety. Stress can also affect mood, contributing to irritability, mood swings, and even symptoms of depression. Cognitive functions may be impacted, leading to memory problems or difficulties with concentration and decision-making. Feelings of overwhelm and a sense of not being able to manage multiple responsibilities effectively are common emotional responses to stress.

Furthermore, individuals in their 40s and beyond may experience social and relational stress, including concerns about loneliness or isolation, as life transitions can sometimes result in changes in social networks. Coping with aging parents' health issues or the loss of loved ones can be emotionally challenging. Balancing career demands and personal life can become more complex, causing stress-related issues in relationships and family dynamics.

Overall, recognizing both the physical and emotional signs of stress in your 40s and beyond is essential for proactive self-care. Addressing stress through mindfulness, relaxation techniques, exercise, and seeking support from friends, family, or mental health professionals can help mitigate these symptoms and promote better overall well-being during this life stage.

Mindfulness Exercises for Symptom Relief

Once you've recognized stress and anxiety, you can perform mindfulness exercises specifically designed to address these symptoms. These exercises are like a soothing balm for your nervous system, helping you find calmness amidst the storm. They'll provide you with practical tools to manage the physical tension, racing thoughts, and emotional turbulence that often accompany stress and anxiety. Some of these we've already discussed, but they're worth mentioning again to specifically combat stress and anxiety.

1. Breathing Exercises: Engage in deep breathing exercises to calm the nervous system. Try the 4-7-8 technique, where you inhale for a count of four, hold for seven, and exhale for eight. Repeat this several times to reduce anxiety and promote relaxation.

2. Body Scan Meditation: Dedicate time to a body scan meditation. Start from your toes and work your way up, paying attention to any areas of tension or discomfort. As you become aware of these sensations, breathe into them and consciously release tension.

3. Mindful Walking: Go for a walk with your full attention on each step. Feel the ground beneath your feet, notice the rhythm of your breath, and observe your surroundings without judgment. Walking mindfully can help clear your mind and reduce stress.

4. Progressive Muscle Relaxation: Practice progressive muscle relaxation by tensing and then releasing different muscle groups in your body. This technique can help you identify and release physical tension.

5. Mindful Eating: Pay close attention to your eating experience. Chew your food slowly, savor the flavors, and notice the texture and smell of your meal. This practice not only promotes healthier eating habits but also helps reduce stress by grounding you in the present moment.

6. Guided Mindfulness Meditation: Use guided mindfulness meditation sessions. Many apps and online resources offer guided meditations specifically designed to reduce stress and anxiety. These can be particularly helpful for those new to meditation.

7. Journaling: Keep a mindfulness journal where you write down your thoughts and feelings, particularly when you're experiencing stress or anxiety. This practice can help you gain insights into your triggers and emotions, leading to better self-awareness.

8. Loving-Kindness Meditation: Practice loving-kindness meditation by sending well-wishes and positive intentions to yourself and others. This practice can promote feelings of compassion and reduce negative emotions associated with stress.

9. Nature Connection: Spend time in nature and practice mindfulness while outdoors. Listen to the sounds of birds, feel the breeze on your skin, and immerse yourself in the natural world, which can be calming and grounding.

10. Yoga: Engage in mindful yoga practices that combine movement and breath awareness. Yoga helps release physical tension and promotes relaxation.

It's essential to be patient with yourself and acknowledge that stress and anxiety may not disappear entirely but can become more manageable through these mindfulness exercises. Additionally, seeking guidance from a mindfulness teacher or therapist can provide valuable support and tailored techniques to address specific stressors and symptoms associated with aging.

Managing Stress in the Moment

When you need quick relief from stress, several strategies can help you regain a sense of calm and composure. First, engage in deep breathing exercises, focusing on slow, deliberate breaths. Inhale deeply through your nose for a count of four, hold for a count of four, and exhale slowly through your mouth for a count of six. This simple technique can activate the body's relaxation response and reduce immediate feelings of tension.

Another effective strategy is grounding yourself in the present moment. Use your senses to connect with your environment by identifying five things you can see, four things you can touch, three things you can hear, two things you can smell, and one thing you can taste. This sensory grounding exercise helps redirect your focus away from stressful thoughts and into the here and now.

Physical activity can also provide quick stress relief. Go for a brisk walk, do a few minutes of stretching, or engage in quick, high-intensity exercise like jumping jacks or push-ups. Physical movement releases endorphins, which are natural mood lifters, and can help dissipate tension and anxiety rapidly.

Lastly, engage in brief mindfulness or meditation exercises. Take just a few minutes to close your eyes, focus on your breath, and bring your attention to the present moment. Acknowledge your thoughts and feelings without judgment, allowing them to come and go. These strategies for quick stress relief can be easily incorporated into your daily routine to help you manage stress as it arises.

Mindful Approaches to Life's Challenges

♥

Navigating life changes mindfully in your 40s and beyond involves embracing a mindset of adaptability and self-compassion. At this stage of life, individuals often encounter significant transitions, such as career shifts, empty nesting, health concerns, or caring for aging parents. Mindfulness can be a valuable tool to navigate these changes effectively.

First, it's crucial to acknowledge the emotions that arise during these transitions. Mindfulness encourages you to observe your thoughts and feelings without judgment. Understand that it's normal to experience fear, uncertainty, or even resistance when facing change. By accepting these emotions, you can begin to respond to them in a more constructive way.

Mindful reflection is also essential. Take time to consider your values, goals, and priorities in light of the changes you're experiencing. This reflection can help you make informed decisions that align with your authentic self rather than reacting impulsively.

Practicing self-compassion is another key aspect. Treat yourself with the same kindness and understanding you would offer to a friend going through a similar transition. Be patient with yourself, recognizing that change is a process, and it's okay to make mistakes or face setbacks along the way.

Maintaining a strong support network is crucial during life changes. Share your thoughts and feelings with trusted friends, family, or a therapist. Their perspectives and emotional support can help you navigate uncertainty more effectively.

Finally, mindfulness practices like meditation, deep breathing, or yoga can provide a sense of stability and calm amidst life's storms. These practices can help you stay present, reduce anxiety, and foster resilience as you navigate the ever-evolving landscape of your 40s and beyond. Ultimately, by approaching life changes mindfully, you can embrace these transitions as opportunities for growth and transformation rather than sources of stress or turmoil.

Applying Mindfulness to Change

Mindfulness provides a stable anchor in the storm of change, helping you navigate these transitions with grace and self-awareness. Let's explore how to navigate specific life changes in one's 40s:

1. Empty-Nesting: When your children leave home and the

nest becomes empty, it's common to experience a mix of emotions, including sadness, loneliness, and uncertainty. Mindfulness encourages you to acknowledge these feelings without judgment. Sit quietly, breathe deeply, and let yourself feel the emotions as they arise. Recognize that these feelings are natural responses to change. Take time to reflect on your values and interests outside your parental role. Mindful journaling can help you explore your goals and aspirations, allowing you to discover new passions or rekindle old ones. Use this time to practice self-care and self-compassion. Engage in activities that nourish your well-being, such as mindfulness meditation, yoga, or hobbies you enjoy. Being present in these moments can help you embrace the newfound freedom that empty nesting brings.

2. Career changes: Practice mindfulness to make informed decisions when contemplating a career change. Reflect on your motivations, strengths, and values. Consider how the change aligns with your long-term goals and whether it contributes to your well-being. As you transition into a new career or role, mindfulness can help you adapt to change more effectively. Embrace the learning process with an open and non-judgmental attitude. Be present in your new environment, observing and absorbing information without rushing to judgments or expectations. Career changes can be stressful, so it's crucial to build resilience. Incorporate mindfulness practices into your daily routine to manage stress, boost confidence, and maintain a healthy work-life balance. Mindful breathing and relaxation techniques can be instrumental during this period of adjustment.

3. Other Major Changes (e.g., divorce, health issues): In the face of significant life changes, such as divorce or health challenges, practice mindfulness to cultivate acceptance. Recognize that change is a part of life, and it's okay to grieve for what was lost. Allow yourself to feel the emotions without suppressing or avoiding them. Seek support from friends, family, or support groups, and practice mindful listening when communicating with others about your experiences. Being fully present in these conversations can aid in connecting with others and receiving the emotional support you need. Use mindfulness techniques, such as body scans or progressive muscle relaxation, to manage the physical and emotional effects of stress related to significant life changes. Mindfulness can help you build resilience and adapt more effectively to new circumstances.

In each of these life changes, mindfulness is a valuable tool to navigate the transitions with greater awareness, self-compassion, and resilience. It allows you to embrace change as an opportunity for personal growth and a chance to cultivate a more fulfilling and mindful life in your 40s and beyond.

Stories of Successful Navigation

Here are some inspiring stories of individuals who have successfully navigated their 40s and beyond.

Jane had spent over two decades in a high-stress corporate job. In her early 40s, she began to experience burnout and realized that her current career path was no longer aligned with her values and well-being. Instead of succumbing to the stress, she decided to embark on a career reinvention journey. Jane explored her passions and discovered a love for holistic wellness and nutrition. She completed certifications in these fields and started her own wellness coaching business.

Jane found renewed purpose and fulfillment in her new career, helping others lead healthier and more balanced lives. Her mindfulness practices, including daily meditation and yoga, have played a crucial role in maintaining her well-being and successfully navigating her 40s and beyond. She now finds joy in her work and embraces the changes that come with age as opportunities for personal growth.

Mark and Sarah had raised their children with dedication and love. As their last child left for college, they faced an empty nest. Rather than feeling empty, they decided to seize the moment and explore their long-held dream of traveling the world. They sold their family home, downsized, and embarked on a journey to visit various countries.

Mark and Sarah's empty nest transition turned into an adventure of a lifetime. They embraced the uncertainty and change with open hearts and minds. Traveling mindfully, they immersed themselves in new cultures, learned new languages, and deepened their connection as a couple. Their 40s and beyond became a time of exploration and discovery, showing that life can be vibrant and exciting during this phase.

These stories illustrate that navigating one's 40s and beyond can lead to successful reinvention and personal growth. By embracing change, pursuing passions, and practicing mindfulness, individuals can find renewed purpose and fulfillment in this stage of life, making it a period of exciting opportunities and meaningful experiences.

Letting Go of Control

The liberating power of acceptance and letting go is at the core of mindfulness practice, offering individuals a profound way to cultivate inner peace and emotional freedom. In mindfulness, acceptance involves acknowledging and embracing the present moment, including one's thoughts, emotions, and circumstances, without judgment or resistance. It's about meeting life as it is rather than as we wish it to be. This radical acceptance allows individuals to break free from the shackles of denial, avoidance, or futile attempts to control everything, which often lead to stress, anxiety, and suffering.

Letting go, in the context of mindfulness, means releasing attachment to thoughts, emotions, and outcomes. It involves recognizing that many struggles arise from our rigid attachment to specific ideas, desires, or expectations. By learning to let go, individuals can unburden themselves from the weight of past regrets or future worries, freeing up mental and emotional energy for the present moment. Letting go doesn't imply indifference but rather a sense of inner peace and resilience, allowing us to respond more skillfully to life's challenges.

Accepting and letting go opens up a profound sense of liberation. It enables individuals to break free from the cycle of rumination and worry, finding solace in the here and now. By accepting their flaws and the world's imperfections, individuals can cultivate self-compassion and compassion for others, fostering deeper connections and reducing interpersonal conflicts. Moreover, the liberating power of acceptance and letting go promotes a sense of flow and adaptability, allowing individuals to navigate life's twists and turns with greater ease and resilience. Mindfulness offers freedom from judgment, attachment, and resistance, leading to a more peaceful and fulfilling existence.

Embracing Life as It Is

Embracing life as it is within the context of mindfulness is a profound practice that involves accepting the present moment without judgment, attachment, or resistance. It's about acknowledging the reality of our circumstances, thoughts, and emotions while cultivating a deep sense of presence and gratitude. Mindfulness encourages us to let go of the constant striving for an idealized future or dwelling on the past and instead find contentment and joy in the here and now.

One key aspect of embracing life as it is involves accepting impermanence. Mindfulness teaches us that everything is constantly changing, including our circumstances, relationships, and even our own bodies. By recognizing this impermanence, we can savor the beauty and preciousness of each moment. This perspective encourages us to let go of unrealistic expectations and find contentment amid life's fluctuations.

Moreover, mindfulness invites us to meet our experiences with an open heart and non-judgmental awareness. We create space for self-compassion and understanding when we approach our thoughts, emotions, and sensations without judgment. This allows us to navigate challenges and difficulties with more resiliency as we learn to respond to them with kindness rather than impulsively.

Embracing life as it is also involves cultivating gratitude. Mindfulness encourages us to notice and appreciate the small joys and blessings that often go unnoticed in our busy lives. By focusing on gratitude, we shift our attention away from what's lacking and redirect it toward what we have, fostering a sense of abundance and contentment.

Mindfulness and Emotional Health

Emotions are an integral part of the human experience, and they can have a profound impact on our well-being. In this chapter, we explore how mindfulness can be a powerful tool for dealing with difficult emotions, allowing you to navigate the ups and downs of life with greater emotional resilience.

Handling Difficult Emotions Mindfully

Handling difficult emotions mindfully in your 40s and beyond involves a combination of self-awareness, self-compassion, and specific mindfulness techniques. First, it's essential to recognize and acknowledge the difficult emotions you're experiencing, whether it's stress, sadness, anxiety, or frustration. Mindfulness encourages you to observe these emotions without judgment or the need to suppress them. Instead of labeling them as "good" or "bad," consider them as natural responses to life's challenges.

Once you've acknowledged these emotions, practice self-compassion. Treat yourself with the same kindness and understanding you would offer to a friend going through a tough time. This self-compassion can help you approach your emotions with gentleness and patience.

Mindfulness techniques, such as mindful breathing or body scans, can be powerful tools to handle difficult emotions. When you notice intense emotions arising, take a moment to focus on your breath and observe the physical sensations associated with the emotion. This helps create a sense of distance between you and the emotion, allowing you to respond more skillfully rather than react impulsively.

Additionally, you can use mindfulness to investigate the underlying causes and triggers of these difficult emotions. By exploring the root of your feelings, you can gain insights into patterns of thinking and behavior that may contribute to emotional distress. This self-awareness can lead to personal growth and healthier ways of managing challenging emotions, making the journey through your 40s and beyond more balanced and fulfilling.

Journaling Prompts and Reflection Exercises. Here are some journaling prompts and reflection exercises to help you handle difficult emotions mindfully:

1. Journaling Prompts:

- What specific emotion am I experiencing right now, and how does it manifest in my body?

- What triggered this emotion? Can I identify any recurring patterns or situations that tend to evoke this feeling?

- How have I typically responded to this emotion in the past, and have those responses been helpful or unhelpful?

- What self-compassionate and nurturing messages can I offer myself in this moment of difficulty?

- What are some positive qualities or strengths that I can draw upon to navigate and manage this emotion effectively?

- How can I reframe my perspective on this emotion? What lessons or insights might it offer me?

- What mindful practices or self-care activities can I engage in to soothe and alleviate the intensity of this emotion?

- What intentions or affirmations can I set for myself to promote emotional well-being and resilience as I move forward?

2. Reflection Exercises:

- **Emotion Awareness Meditation:** Dedicate a few minutes to sit in a quiet space, close your eyes, and bring your attention to the emotion you're currently grappling with. Observe the sensations it creates in your body without judgment. Allow the emotion to be present and breathe into it with kindness and curiosity.

- **Emotion Timeline:** Create a timeline of your life, highlighting significant emotional events or challenges you've faced in your 40s and beyond. Reflect on how you navigated these situations and the emotional growth you've experienced.

- **Letter to Your Younger Self:** Write a letter to your younger self, offering guidance and wisdom on how to handle difficult emotions. Consider the advice you wish you had received at that age and how it might have helped you in your 40s and beyond.

- **Mindful Gratitude Practice:** Reflect on moments in your life when you successfully managed difficult emotions and emerged stronger. Express gratitude for your resilience and the growth these experiences have brought you.

- **Self-Compassion Exercise:** Write a letter of self-compassion to yourself, addressing the difficult emotion you're currently facing. Imagine you are offering comfort and support to a dear friend experiencing the same emotion. This exercise can foster self-compassion and self-kindness.

- **Emotion Journal:** Keep an emotion journal where you regularly record your emotional experiences. Note the triggers, physical sensations, and thoughts associated with each emotion. This journal can help you identify patterns and develop mindful strategies for handling difficult emotions more effectively.

These journaling prompts and reflection exercises can assist in developing greater emotional awareness and resilience while navigating the complexities of life's challenges.

Cultivating Positive Emotions

While mindfulness helps us address difficult emotions, it also empowers us to cultivate positive ones. One key approach is cultivating gratitude. Take time each day to reflect on what you're thankful for, whether it's your health, relationships, accomplishments, or the simple pleasures in life. Gratitude practices can shift your focus towards the positive aspects of your life, promoting a more optimistic outlook.

Engaging in activities that bring you joy is another effective method. Reconnect with hobbies or interests you may have set aside over the years. Pursue new experiences and adventures, whether traveling to new destinations, learning a new skill, or taking up a creative endeavor. These activities can stimulate feelings of enthusiasm, excitement, and satisfaction.

Nurturing strong social connections is crucial for emotional well-being. Invest time in your relationships with friends and family, as meaningful connections provide a sense of belonging and support. Building and maintaining a support network can offer opportunities for laughter, shared experiences, and a sense of camaraderie, all of which contribute to positive emotions. Lastly, practicing mindfulness and self-compassion can help you manage negative emotions and increase your overall emotional resilience, allowing you to approach life's challenges with a positive and balanced mindset.

Cultivating daily habits for positivity is a powerful way to enhance your overall well-being and mindset. Start your day with a morning routine that includes mindfulness or meditation. Dedicate a few minutes to focus on your breath, express gratitude, or set positive intentions for the day ahead. This practice can help you start the day with a clear and positive mindset.

Throughout the day, practice self-compassion and self-care. Treat yourself with kindness, especially in moments of self-doubt or criticism. Take short breaks to stretch, breathe deeply, or enjoy a mindful cup of tea. Prioritize physical activity, as exercise releases endorphins, promoting a sense of well-being and positivity.

Maintain a gratitude journal to record the things you appreciate daily. Reflect on the positive moments, no matter how small they may seem. This practice helps shift your focus towards the positive aspects of life. Surround yourself with positivity by spending time with supportive and uplifting people. Engage in activities that bring joy and fulfillment, and consider limiting exposure to negative news or content that can affect your mood. Ultimately, cultivating daily habits for positivity is about consciously choosing actions and thoughts that promote a positive outlook on life.

Mindful Aging

♥

E**mbracing Aging.** Accepting aging gracefully in your 40s involves embracing change and nurturing a positive mindset. Begin by acknowledging the natural progression of time and the physical changes that come with it. Instead of resisting or denying these changes, cultivate self-compassion and self-acceptance. Focus on your inner qualities, experiences, and wisdom gained over the years, appreciating the unique journey that has brought you to this point.

Engage in self-care practices that prioritize your well-being, both physically and emotionally. Surround yourself with supportive relationships and maintain a solid social network. By fostering resilience, gratitude, and a mindful approach to life, you can navigate your 40s with grace and acceptance, realizing that aging is a beautiful part of the human experience.

Positive Mindset about Getting Older

Maintaining a positive mindset on aging in your 40s is crucial for overall well-being. It involves shifting your perspective from fearing the passage of time to embracing the opportunities it brings. Recognize that each year adds depth to your life experiences and wisdom to your character. Instead of fixating on external appearances, focus on your inner growth, resilience, and the meaningful connections you've cultivated. A positive mindset allows you to approach your 40s with gratitude, appreciating the journey and looking forward to the possibilities ahead, as aging becomes a source of strength and personal evolution. Remember that age is not just a number; it reflects the wisdom and experiences you've accumulated over the years.

Mindfulness for Longevity

Regular mindfulness practices can contribute to a longer, healthier life. Firstly, it helps reduce stress, significantly contributing to various health issues. Chronic stress can lead to inflammation, cardiovascular problems, and weakened immune function. Mindfulness practices like meditation and deep breathing exercises activate the body's relaxation response, lowering stress hormones and promoting a sense of calm, thereby reducing the wear and tear on the body.

Secondly, mindfulness encourages healthy lifestyle choices. Enhancing self-awareness makes individuals more likely to make conscious decisions regarding their diet, exercise, and overall well-being. Mindful eating, for instance, can lead to better food choices, portion control, and improved digestion. This, in turn, supports physical health and contributes to longevity.

Lastly, mindfulness can enhance the quality of life as people age. Cultivating a present-focused and appreciative attitude helps individuals find joy and contentment in everyday experiences, fostering positive emotions and resilience. Emotional well-being is associated with better health outcomes and a longer life. In sum, mindfulness promotes longevity by reducing stress, promoting healthy behaviors, and enhancing emotional well-being, contributing to a longer and more fulfilling life.

Staying Mentally Sharp and Focused

Mindfulness can help individuals aged 40 and older maintain mental sharpness and focus by strengthening cognitive abilities and enhancing attention control. Regular mindfulness practice, such as meditation, challenges the brain to stay present and alert, improving concentration and memory. It also fosters self-awareness, enabling individuals to notice distractions and mind-wandering more quickly, allowing them to redirect their focus to the task. Additionally, mindfulness reduces stress and promotes emotional resilience, which can help prevent cognitive decline and age-related cognitive disorders. By nurturing mental clarity and cognitive flexibility, mindfulness supports overall cognitive health as individuals age.

Advanced Mindfulness Practices

♥

For those readers who have embarked on their mindfulness journey and are ready to take it to the next level, this chapter introduces more advanced mindfulness techniques to help you deepen your practice. We'll also explore the path of becoming a lifelong mindfulness practitioner.

Advanced Mindfulness Techniques. These techniques are designed to challenge and expand your awareness, taking you deeper into mindfulness. Whether exploring different meditation styles, incorporating mindful movement, or engaging in advanced breathwork, you'll have a range of tools to choose from to deepen your practice.

Advanced mindfulness techniques are suitable for individuals who have already established a regular mindfulness practice and are ready to deepen their awareness and insights. Here are some advanced techniques to consider:

1. Vipassana Meditation: Vipassana is an ancient meditation practice that involves observing the sensations in the body with deep awareness. Practitioners systematically scan their bodies and mindfully explore physical and mental sensations, gaining profound insights into the impermanent and interconnected nature of all experiences.

2. Loving-kindness Meditation: This practice involves cultivating boundless love and compassion for oneself and others. Advanced practitioners can extend loving-kindness to challenging individuals or even to all sentient beings, expanding their capacity for unconditional love and empathy.

3. Body Scan Meditation: Take body scanning to the next level by intensifying your focus. Explore sensations at a micro-level, zooming in on each part of the body and observing even the subtlest sensations and energy flows. This deepens the connection between body and mind.

4. Mindful Observation: Engage in deep mindfulness by observing everyday objects or natural phenomena with unwavering attention. Explore the essence of each moment, whether it's a flower, a candle flame, or a raindrop sliding down a window.

5. Silent Retreats: Consider attending a silent meditation retreat, which can last several days or even weeks. This immersive experience allows you to deepen your practice, as the absence of external distractions fosters continuous mindful-

ness.

6. Koan Meditation: In Zen Buddhism, koans are paradoxical statements or questions that transcend logical thinking. Advanced practitioners work with koans to break down conceptual boundaries and attain deeper insights into the nature of reality.

These advanced mindfulness techniques require patience, dedication, and guidance from experienced teachers. It's essential to approach them with humility and a genuine desire for spiritual growth, as they can lead to profound transformations in your understanding of self and the world.

The Lifelong Journey

Mindfulness is not just a temporary practice; it's a lifelong journey. Becoming a lifelong mindfulness practitioner requires a mindset of patience, openness, and continuous learning. It's a commitment to cultivating self-awareness and inner peace, not as a destination but as an ongoing journey. One must be willing to embrace both the challenges and the rewards that mindfulness offers, understanding that progress may be gradual and non-linear. It involves a dedication to daily practice, even during busy or difficult times, and seeking guidance from experienced teachers and a supportive community. Ultimately, the commitment to lifelong mindfulness is about nurturing a deep connection with the present moment and an unwavering intention to live with mindfulness as an integral part of one's life.

Mindfulness Retreats and Workshops

Immersive experiences can provide profound opportunities for growth and transformation in your mindfulness practice. Whether it's a silent meditation retreat, a mindfulness-based stress reduction (MBSR) workshop, or a nature-based mindfulness retreat, follow these five guidelines on selecting the right retreat or workshop for you:

1. Define Your Objectives: Start by clarifying your intentions and goals for the mindfulness workshop or retreat. Are you seeking stress reduction, emotional healing, deeper self-awareness, or advanced meditation techniques? Understanding your objectives will guide your selection process.

2. Research Mindfulness Programs: Conduct thorough research by exploring various mindfulness programs available. Utilize online resources, mindfulness websites, social media, and recommendations from others in the mindfulness community. Look for programs that match your goals and preferences.

3. Evaluate Program Details: Once you've identified potential workshops or retreats, evaluate the program details.

- Program Focus: Consider the specific focus of the program, whether it's mindfulness-based stress reduction, mindfulness meditation, loving-kindness meditation, or a specialized retreat like mindful eating or nature immersion.

- Duration and Format: Assess the program's length, daily schedule, and format. Decide whether you prefer shorter workshops, week-long retreats, silent or guided experiences and whether you can commit to the duration.

- Location and Logistics: Consider the location, accommodation options, cost, and available dates. Ensure that the location is accessible and aligns with your budget and schedule.

4. Research Instructors: Investigate the instructors' or facilitators' qualifications and teaching backgrounds. Experienced and well-trained instructors can significantly enhance your learning experience. Learn about their teaching philosophy and approach to mindfulness.

5. Seek Reviews and Recommendations: Look for reviews, testimonials, or recommendations from individuals who have attended the same mindfulness program. Hearing about their firsthand experiences can provide valuable insights into the program's quality and effectiveness.

Experiences from Practitioners

Here are some firsthand perspectives from individuals who have deepened their mindfulness practices through immersive experiences:

- Lucy's Silent Retreat Experience: Lucy, a 45-year-old professional, attended a 10-day silent meditation retreat in a remote mountain retreat center. She described it as a transformative experience. "The silence allowed me to truly connect with my inner self," she said. "Without the usual distractions, I became acutely aware of my thoughts and emotions. Over those days, I learned to observe them without judgment, which was incredibly liberating. It helped me break free from old patterns and be more present in my everyday life."

- Carlos's Mindful Nature Retreat: Carlos, a 50-year-old nature enthusiast, joined a mindful nature retreat in a forested area. He shared, "Being surrounded by the beauty of nature, I felt a profound sense of interconnectedness. The guided meditations and nature walks helped me cultivate a deep appreciation for the environment. I left the retreat with a heightened sense of gratitude and a newfound commitment to environmental stewardship."

- Sara's Mindful Eating Workshop: Sara, a 38-year-old nutritionist, attended a mindful eating workshop. She noted, "The workshop taught me to savor every bite and pay attention to my body's hunger and fullness cues. I realized how often I used to eat mindlessly. Now, I approach meals with a sense of mindfulness and gratitude, which has not only improved my relationship with food but also my overall well-being."

- David's Advanced Meditation Retreat: David, a 55-year-old experienced meditator, attended an advanced meditation retreat led by a renowned teacher. "The deepening of my practice was profound," he shared. "I learned advanced techniques and gained insights into the nature of the mind. The teachings challenged me in the best possible way, pushing me beyond my comfort zone and deepening my understanding of meditation."

These firsthand experiences illustrate how immersive mindfulness retreats and workshops can profoundly impact individuals, leading to increased self-awareness, a deeper connection with nature, improved relationships with food, and advanced meditation skills. These transformative experiences often motivate individuals to continue their mindfulness journeys with renewed enthusiasm and dedication.

Integrating Mindfulness into Your Legacy

♥

As you near the end of this transformative journey, it's time to contemplate how mindfulness can become an enduring legacy that you pass on to future generations. In this chapter, we'll inspire you to consider how you can embody mindfulness principles in all aspects of life and inspire others to do the same.

Inspiring Others with Mindful Living. Embracing mindfulness is not only a journey of personal growth but also an opportunity to positively influence those around you. As you experience the profound benefits of mindfulness in your own life, consider how you can pass on these invaluable gifts to others. Start by setting an example through your own practice. By embodying mindfulness principles in your daily life—whether it's staying present in conversations, managing stress with grace, or nurturing a compassionate outlook—you inspire those around you to do the same.

Another way to share the benefits of mindfulness is by introducing it to friends, family, or colleagues. You can organize mindfulness sessions, recommend books or apps, or engage in open conversations about your experiences. You empower others to embark on their own mindfulness journey by providing resources and guidance. Moreover, creating a supportive community or joining mindfulness groups can foster a sense of connection and shared growth, amplifying the positive impact.

Lastly, consider extending mindfulness beyond your immediate circle through volunteer work or outreach programs. Many organizations offer mindfulness training to underserved communities, schools, or healthcare settings. By contributing your time and knowledge, you can help individuals from all walks of life access mindfulness's healing and transformative power. In doing so, you become a beacon of inspiration, spreading the profound benefits of mindfulness to those who may need it most, creating a ripple effect of positive change in the world.

Embodying Mindfulness in All Aspects of Life. Embodying mindfulness principles in all aspects of life requires a conscious and deliberate commitment to present-moment awareness and a compassionate presence. To begin, start by integrating mindfulness into everyday activities. Whether you're eating, walking, or doing household chores, bring your full attention to the task at hand. Notice the sensory experiences, thoughts, and emotions that arise without judgment, allowing them to come and go like passing clouds.

Mindfulness extends beyond individual actions; it also involves nurturing mindful relationships. Practice active listening by giving your full attention to others when they speak, without rushing to formulate responses. Cultivate empathy and understanding, allowing for open and non-judgmental communication. In conflicts or disagreements, approach conversations with mindfulness, seeking solutions based on understanding and compassion rather than reactivity.

Furthermore, extend mindfulness to your inner world by observing your thoughts and emotions with curiosity and kindness. Rather than identifying with them, view them as passing phenomena. Develop a daily mindfulness meditation practice to strengthen your ability to stay grounded in the present moment. By consistently applying these principles in your daily life, you cultivate a deeper sense of awareness, compassion, and inner peace, ultimately embodying mindfulness as a way of being, not just a technique.

Teaching Mindfulness to the Next Generation. Introducing mindfulness practices to children and grandchildren can be a beautiful gift that helps them navigate life's challenges with greater resilience and presence. Begin by setting a personal example through your own mindfulness practice. Children often learn best by observing adults, so let them see you incorporate mindfulness into your daily routine, whether through meditation, mindful breathing, or simply being fully present in their company.

Make mindfulness playful and engaging to capture their interest. Use age-appropriate resources like books, games, or guided meditations designed for kids. Create opportunities for mindful activities together, such as nature walks, mindful coloring, or simple breathing exercises. Be patient and open to their questions and experiences, allowing them to explore mindfulness at their own pace. Cultivating mindfulness in the younger generation can provide them with lifelong skills for managing stress, developing emotional intelligence, and fostering a sense of well-being.

Family-Friendly Mindfulness Activities and Education. Family-friendly mindfulness activities and education can be a wonderful way to foster a sense of calm and connection within your household. Several resources and tools are available to help you introduce mindfulness to your family:

1. Mindfulness Apps: There are various mindfulness apps designed for children and families. Apps like "Calm for Kids," "Headspace for Kids," and "Smiling Mind" offer guided meditations and activities suitable for different age groups.

2. Books: Many mindfulness books are tailored for kids, making it easier to explain the concepts to them. Look for titles like "Sitting Still Like a Frog" by Eline Snel, "The Mindful Dragon" by Steve Herman, or "Breathe Like a Bear" by Kira Willey, which combine storytelling and mindfulness exercises.

3. YouTube Channels: Several YouTube channels offer family-friendly mindfulness content. Channels like "Cosmic Kids Yoga" and "Mindful Schools" provide guided practices, yoga sessions, and mindful storytelling.

4. Online Courses: Consider enrolling in online mindfulness courses designed for families. Organizations like Mindful Schools offer family programs that teach mindfulness techniques suitable for both parents and children.

5. Local Classes and Workshops: Check for mindfulness classes or workshops in your community, many of which cater to families. These in-person experiences can provide a shared learning environment and community support.

Remember that introducing mindfulness to your family is a journey of exploration and growth. Start with resources that resonate with your family's needs and interests, and adapt the practices to suit your unique dynamics. You can create a harmonious and mindful family environment by fostering mindfulness together.

Conclusion

As you reach the end of this transformative journey through "Mindfulness and Mental Health: Staying Balanced and Focused in Your 40s and Beyond," let's summarize the key takeaways from the book.

1. Mindfulness as a Lifelong Companion: Mindfulness is not just a passing trend; it's a lifelong companion that can support you through the unique challenges of your 40s and beyond. It offers tools for maintaining balance, resilience, and emotional well-being.

2. Embracing Change: Your 40s and beyond bring changes, transitions, and challenges. Mindfulness equips you to navigate these with grace and acceptance, helping you find wisdom and growth in the face of uncertainty.

3. Emotional Well-Being: Mindfulness empowers you to understand, process, and embrace your emotions, whether they are difficult or positive. It offers techniques for managing stress and anxiety while cultivating a positive mindset.

4. Mindful Aging: Aging is an opportunity for growth, and mindfulness can help you embrace it with grace. It promotes longevity, mental sharpness, and a positive outlook on getting older.

5. Legacy of Mindfulness: Mindful living can become a lasting legacy, inspiring those around you to embark on their mindfulness journey. Teaching mindfulness to the next generation ensures that the benefits continue to ripple through time.

Final Words of Encouragement

As you navigate your 40s and beyond, mindfulness becomes an invaluable companion on your journey of self-discovery, personal growth, and well-being. This stage of life brings its own set of challenges and opportunities, and practicing mindfulness can be a source of profound strength and clarity.

Embrace the wisdom that comes with age, and let mindfulness be your guide. It allows you to savor the present moment, appreciating the richness of life's experiences, whether it's a quiet morning sunrise or a cherished conversation with a loved one. You can find more profound contentment and fulfillment in the simple joys surrounding you by grounding yourself in the here and now.

In this stage of life, you may also encounter increased stress, responsibilities, and uncertainties. Mindfulness equips you with the tools to manage these challenges gracefully. It fosters emotional resilience, helping you navigate life's inevitable ups and downs with a steadiness that comes from within.

Moreover, mindfulness encourages self-compassion and self-care. As you juggle various roles and responsibilities, remember that taking time for yourself is not selfish; it's a necessity. You can find tranquility and rejuvenation through mindfulness practices like meditation and deep breathing, nurturing your mental and emotional well-being.

Incorporating mindfulness into your daily life in this phase can lead to a profound sense of fulfillment and purpose, ensuring that your journey through your 40s and beyond is one of growth, wisdom, and deep inner peace. So, take a moment, breathe, and embrace the path of mindfulness as your lifelong companion.

Lastly, as you move through your 40s and beyond, remember that growth and transformation are lifelong processes. Embrace change with an open heart and mind, as mindfulness teaches us to accept what is and adapt gracefully. Continue to explore, learn, and evolve, knowing that each day is an opportunity to become more present, more resilient, and more in tune with your authentic self.

Resources for Continued Learning and Practice

To continue your mindfulness journey, here is a list of resources:

- **Books:**

- *The Miracle of Mindfulness* by Thich Nhat Hanh

- *Radical Acceptance* by Tara Brach

- *The Power of Now* by Eckhart Tolle

- **Apps:**

- Headspace

- Calm

- Insight Timer

  - **Online Courses:**

- Mindfulness-Based Stress Reduction (MBSR) programs

- Mindful Self-Compassion (MSC) courses

  - **Retreats and Workshops:** Explore local or virtual mindfulness retreats and workshops to deepen your practice. You can also join local meditation groups or mindfulness communities to connect with like-minded individuals.

Remember that your mindfulness journey is a lifelong adventure filled with discoveries, challenges, and profound moments of clarity. It's a path that leads to greater well-being, deeper self-awareness, and a more meaningful life. May you continue to walk this path with curiosity, compassion, and an open heart.

www.ingramcontent.com/pod-product-compliance
Lightning Source LLC
LaVergne TN
LVHW052002060526
838201LV00059B/3794